Greek for Beginners
BY GETAWAY GUIDES

The Best Handbook for Learning to Speak Greek!
2nd Edition

Greek for Beginners

Copyright 2014 by Getaway Guides - All rights reserved.

In no way is it legal to reproduce, duplicate, or transmit any part of this document in either electronic means or in printed format. Recording of this publication is strictly prohibited and any storage of this document is not allowed unless with written permission from the publisher. All rights reserved.

Table of Contents

Introduction 4
Chapter 1: The Greek Alphabet and Pronunciation 5
Chapter 2: Parts of Speech 10
Chapter 3: Tenses of Verbs 13
Chapter 4: Greek Grammar 101 17
Chapter 5: Basic Phrases 21
Chapter 6: Getting a Room 23
Chapter 7: Getting Around 25
Chapter 8: Food and Drinks 27
Chapter 9: Shopping Around 29
Chapter 10: Other Useful Words and Phrases 31
Chapter 11: Romantic Phrases 35
Chapter 12: Exercises to Improve Your Communication Skills 36
Conclusion 38
Check Out My Other Books 39

Introduction

I want to thank you and congratulate you for purchasing the book, *"Greek for Beginners: The Best Handbook for Learning to Speak Greek!"*

Greece is said to be the birthplace of the Western Civilization and the Greek Language dates back to 1400 BC and is currently spoken by over 13 million people worldwide. Aside from those who live in Greece, Greek is also spoken by some people in Albania, Cyprus, Armenia, Romania, Georgia, Israel, Southern Italy, Brazil, Argentina and Austria, among others.

With Greece's colorful history comes a colorful language that's truly worth learning—and that's what you are going to experience right now. While it may not be as easy as other languages to learn, it is still very useful especially if you find yourself in a Greek-speaking country. It's just respectful that you learn different languages so you can easily converse with different kinds of people.

With the help of this book, learning to speak Greek wouldn't be as hard as you think it is.

Start flipping the pages and be fluent in Greek in no time!

Thanks again for purchasing this book. I hope you enjoy it!

Chapter 1: The Greek Alphabet and Pronunciation

The Greek alphabet has almost the same number of letters as the English alphabet. To speak Greek, you have to learn the letters and their pronunciation. Below are the letters that make up the Greek Alphabet, their English Translations, and their pronunciations according to their nearest English equivalent:

Letter	Phonetic equivalent	Pronounced as
➢ A α – Alpha	à	**a** in f**a**ther
➢ B β – Beta	v	**v** in **v**ictory
➢ Γ γ – Gamma	y, y	**y** in **y**es
➢ Δ δ – Delta	**th**	**th** in **th**ey
➢ E ε – Epsilon	ĕ	**e** in r**e**d
➢ Z ζ – Zeta	z	**z** in **z**ero
➢ H η – Eta	ï, ĭ	**i** in **i**ll or mach**i**ne
➢ Θ θ – Theta	th	**th** in **th**in
➢ I ι – Iota	ï, ĭ	**i** in **i**ll or mach**i**ne
➢ K κ – Kappa	k	**k** in **k**ing
➢ Λ λ – Lambda	l	**l** in **l**ot
➢ M μ – mu	m	**m** in **m**other
➢ N ν – nu	n	**n** in **n**ow
➢ Ξ ξ – xi	x, ks	**x** in e**x**tra
➢ O o – Omicron	o	**o** in c**o**rporal
➢ Π π – Pi	p	**p** in **p**aper
➢ P ρ (or sometimes б) – Rho	r	**r** in **r**ed
➢ Σ σ ς – Sigma	s	**s** in **s**ister
➢ T τ – Tau	t	**t** in **t**in
➢ Y υ – Upsilon	ï, ĭ	**i** in **i**ll or mach**i**ne
➢ Φ φ – Phi	f	**f** in **f**at

Greek for Beginners

- X x – Chi   h   **h** in **h**ill (aspirated)
- Ψ ψ – Psi   ps   **ps** in li**ps**
- Ω ώ – Omega   o   **o** in c**o**rporal

Notes:

- Γ, γ – The sound of **γ** can be correctly learned only by listening to a Greek. It is a soft, guttural **g**, equivalent to the consonant sound of **y** in **year** or **yellow**, or the sound of **w** in **woman**. Before the vowels **α, ο**, or **ω** and the diphthong **ου, γ** can be likened to the consonant sound of **y** in **yard** or **yoke**. It would not be correct to represent it in all cases with **y** or **w** or **g**. Therefore, in the phonetic pronunciation, we have mostly retained its Greek character **γ**:

    Γάτα   γá'tà   cat

    γγ and **γκ** are pronounced as **ng** in **longer** or **angry**:

    γεμᾶτος   ěng'gonos   grandson

    αγκάλη   àngá'lĭ   bosom

    γ before the consonants **χ** or **ξ** is pronounced as **ng** nasal, as in **song**:

    συγχορῶ   sĭng horo'   I pardon

    πλάστιγξ   plás'tĭngks   scales

- Σ, σ, ς – This is pronounced as **s** in **sister**. Before the consonants **β, γ, δ, λ, μ, ν** and **ρ**, it takes the sound of z, which is considered more euphonious:

    σῠστημα   sï'stĭmà   system

    κόσμος   koz'mos   world

    σανίς   sànïs'   board

    ασβεστος   àz'věstos   lime

- Χ, χ – This is a guttural consonant pronounced as a heavily aspirated **h**. The correct sound of **χ** should be learned from a Greek. It has no equivalent in English. It is similar to the German **ch** in **Bach**.

- Gamma and Kappa are usually used with only one consonant.

- Small Sigma (ς) is used only at the end of a word; that is why it is often called *final sigma*. It's also sometimes used as a symbol for a small crescent moon.
- The alphabet can also be used as numerals, which are as follows:
  - Alpha - 1
  - Beta - 2
  - Gamma - 3
  - Delta - 4
  - Epsilon – 5
  - Digamma/Stigma - 6
  - Zeta - 7
  - Eta – 8
  - Theta – 9
  - Iota – 10
  - Kappa – 20
  - Lambda – 30
  - Mu – 50
  - Nu - 60
  - Omicron – 70
  - Pi – 80
  - Koppa - 90
  - Rho – 100
  - Sigma – 200
  - Tau – 300
  - Upsilon – 400
  - Phi – 500
  - Chi – 600

- Psi – 700
- Omega – 800
- Sampi – 900
- Khilioi - 1000

Dipthongs (Two Vowels Pronounced as One)

α ι is pronounced as ĕ: αίμα (ĕ'mȧ) blood.

ε ι, ο ι, and υ ι are pronounced as ĭ or ï:

ε ί ν α ι	(ï'ne)	is
οίνος	(ĭnos)	wine
υιός	(ĭ os')	son.

ο υ is pronounced as oo:

| ο ὐ ρ α ν ό ς | (oorȧnos') | sky. |

α υ, ε υ, and η υ are pronounced as ȧv, ĕv, and ĭv, respectively. But if followed by the consonants θ, κ, ξ, π, σ, τ, or ψ, they are pronounced as ȧf, ĕf, and ĭf, respectively. Examples:

α ὐ γ ή	(ȧv γĭ')	dawn
α ὐ τ ό ς	(ȧf tos')	he
ε ὐ ή λ ι ο ς	(ĕvï'lĭos)	sunny
ε ὐ θ ύ ς	(ĕf thïs')	immediately

Accents and Punctuation Marks

Three accents are used in the Greek language:

- **acute** (´) – used on one of the last three syllable. For example:

    μ έ λ ι σ σ α   κ ά μ ν ω

- **grave** (`) – used on the last syllable. For example:

    κ α λ ὸ ς   π α τ ὴ ρ

- **circumflex** (˜) – used on either of the last two syllables. For example:

μῆλον					ἀγαπῶ

Greek punctuation marks are the same as in English, except the semicolon which is represented by a high period (·) and the interrogation mark represented by a semicolon (;).

Chapter 2: Parts of Speech

In English, we have different parts of speech: nouns, pronouns, verbs, adverbs, adjectives, etc. This chapter deals with the basics of Greek parts of speech, which in the later chapters will help you express yourself better in the language.

Genders and Articles

There are three genders in Greek: masculine, feminine and neuter. Inasmuch as there are no rules for distinguishing the gender, we denote it with the definite article before each noun.

The definite article is **o** for the masculine, **η** for the feminine and **τὸ** for the neuter gender. For example:

ο πατέρας	the father
η μητέρα	the mother
τὸ παιδὶ	the child

The indefinite article is **ε ν α ς** for the masculine, **μ ί α** for the feminine and **ε ν α** for the neuter gender—all meaning **one**:

ενας πατέρας	a father
μία μητέρα	a mother
ενα παιδὶ	a child

Both the definite and indefinite articles are declined or change form according to cases and numbers, as we shall learn later.

In Greek, the definite article is usually placed before a proper name:

Ο Γιάννης	(The) John
Η Μαρία	(The) Mary
Τὸν Γεώργιον	(The) George

Personal Pronouns

εγώ	I
σὐ	you (singular)

α υ τ ό ς	he
α υ τ ὴ	she
α υ τ ό	it
η μ ε ῖ ς (or colloquially, ε μ ε ῖ ς)	we
σ ε ῖ ς	you (plural)
α υ τ ο ὶ	they (masculine)
α υ τ α ί (or colloquially, α υ τ έ ς)	they (feminine)
α υ τ ὰ	they (neuter)

Note: In Greek, the second person singular is used when speaking to persons with whom one is familiar. The second person plural is used only when politeness or formality is desired to be shown.

The third personal pronouns **α υ τ ό ς, α υ τ ὴ**, and **α υ τ ό** (he, she, it) also serve as adverbs and are declined likewise. For example:

Α υ τ ό ς α ν θ ρ ω π ο ς	This man
Α υ τ ο ὶ α ν θ ρ ω π ο ι	These men, these people
Α υ τ ὴ η κ ό ρ η	This girl
Α υ τ α ί α ι κ ό ρ α ι	These girls
Α υ τ ὸ τ ο π α ι δ ι	This child
Α υ τ ὰ τ ὰ π α ι δ ι ά	This children

Pronouns and Verbs

Greek verbs are not necessarily preceded or followed by personal pronouns as in English. The change of the last syllable indicates the person of the verb. For example:

Ε χ ω	I have
Ε χ ε ι ς	You have
Ε χ ε ι	He has, she has, it has

Adjectives

Adjectives in Greek change form according to the gender, case and number of the nouns of the nouns they qualify.

Most adjectives end in **ο ς** for the masculine, **α** or the **η** for the feminine and **ο ν** (or abbreviated **ο**) for the neuter gender. For example:

Ο καλὸς πατερας	The good father
Η καλὴ μητέρα	The good mother
Τὸ καλὸν παιδίον	The good boy
or colloquially, Τὸ καλὸ παιδίο	
Κακὸς ἄωθρωπος	Bad man
Κακὴ γυναῖκα	Bad woman
Κακὸν πρᾶγμα	Bad thing
(or colloquially, κακὸ)	

Adverbs from Adjectives

Adverbs are formed from adjectives with the ending **α** (and in the puristic language **ω ς**):

καταρός – καθαρά (or καθαρῶς)	clean – cleanly
κακός – κακά (or κακῶς)	bad – badly
καλὸς – καλὰ (or καλῶς)	good – well
ὠραῖος – ωραῖα	beautiful – beautifully
γρήγορος – γρήγορα	quick – quickly

Chapter 3: Tenses of Verbs

Past Tense of Verbs

In Greek verbs, there are three past tenses in use: the **Imperfect** or **Continued Past** tense, the **Aorist** or **Indefinite Past** tense, and the **Perfect** or **Compound Past** tense.

Though there are some rules for the formation of the past tenses of the regular verbs, yet there are so many exceptions and irregularities, especially among verbs of the most common use, that we have found it preferable to give with each verb its present and past tenses. From these, all the other tenses and moods can be easily formed, as we shall learn later.

In the continued past and indefinite past tenses the vowel **ε** is placed before verbs beginning with a consonant. Also, the accent is raised from the second to the third syllable from the end. Examples:

Present	Continued Past	Indefinite Past
δ ί δ ω	ε δ ι δ α	ε δ ο σ α (or ε δ ω σ α)
I give	I was giving,	I gave
	I used to give	
κ ά μ ν ω	ε χ α μ ν α	ε κ α μ α
I do	I was doing,	I did
	I used to do	
φ έ ρ ω	ε φ ε ρ α	ε φ ε ρ α
I bring	I was bringing,	I brought
	I used to bring	

The Perfect Past Tense, as in English, is formed with the auxiliary **ε χ ω** (I have) and the perfect past form of the verb ending in **ε ι** (or **η**). Examples:

Κ ά μ ν ω	I do
Ε χ ω κ ά μ ε ι	I have done
Ε χ ε ι ς κ ά μ ε ι	You have done (singular.)

Εχει κάμει	He (she, it) has done
Εχομεν κάμει	We have done
Εχετε κάμει	You have done
Εχουν κάμει	They have done

In the same manner, the Pluperfect Tense is formed with the auxiliary **ε ῖ χ α** (I had) and the verb ending in **ε ι** or **η**. For example:

Εῖχα κάμει	I had done
Εῖχε ςκάμει	You had done (singular)
Εῖχε κάμει	He (she, it) had done
Εῖχαμεν κάμει	We had done
Εῖχατε κάμεν	You had done
Εῖχαν κάμει	They had done

Future Tenses

Two future tenses are used in Modem Greek: a) The Continuous Future Tense and b) the Momentary Future Tense.

The Continuous Future Tense is the verb in its present tense preceded by the auxiliary word **θ ὰ**. For example:

Θὰ δίδω	I shall be giving (or I shall give)
Θὰ δίδεις	You will be giving
Θὰ δίδει	He (she, it) will be giving
Θὰ δίδομεν	We shall be giving

The Momentary Future is formed with the auxiliary **θ ὰ** and the verb in its momentary form. Examples:

Κάμνω	I do
Εχω κάμει	I have done
Θὰ κάμω	I shall do
Θὰ κάμεις	You will do
Θὰ κάμει	He (she, it) will do

Θὰ κάμομεν	We shall do
Θὰ κάμετε	You will do
Θὰ κάμουν	They will do
Βλέπω	I see
Εχω ιδες (or ιδει)	I have seen
Θὰ ιδω	I shall see
Θὰ ιδεις	You will see
Θὰ ιδει	He (she, it) will see
Θὰ ιδομεν	We shall see
Θὰ ιδετε	You will see
Θὰ ιδουν	They will see

Similar to the auxiliary word **θὰ** (will) is the auxiliary word **νὰ** (to) with which the Subjunctive mood of verbs is formed. The verb may be either in continuous or momentary form. Examples:

Θέλω νὰ κάμω	I want to do
Θελεις νὰ κάμης	You want to do

In Modern Greek verbs, two basic forms are used: one signifying **continuity**, and the other expressing **momentary** action. Thus there are a continuous past and a momentary past tense, a continuous future and a momentary future tense, a continuous imperative and a momentary imperative mood, a continuous subjunctive and a momentary subjunctive. However, in the present indicative tense the same form is used for expressing both continuous and momentary action, or condition. Examples:

Momentary	**Continuous**
PRESENT	
Δίδω — I give	Δίδω — I am giving
PAST	
Εδωσα — I gave	Εδιδον, εδιδα — I was giving
FUTURE	
Θα δώσω — I shall give	θὰ διδω — I shall be giving

IMPERATIVE

Δῶσε or Δόσε — Give   Δίδε — Give (be giving)

SUBJUNCTIVE

Νὰ δώσω — To give   Νὰ δίδω – To give (to be giving)

Greek for Beginners

Chapter 4: Greek Grammar 101

Now that you know the alphabet and parts of speech, it's time to express yourself. In this chapter, you will learn the basics of Greek grammar and hence develop simple statements. As you learn how the example words are carefully chosen and arranged, try to pronounce them well. To make your study of Greek easier, we suggest that you accompany this guide with a Greek-English dictionary. By the end of this chapter you should have an adequate understanding of Greek. So let's begin!

Structure of Simple Sentence

In Greek, it is not required to place the subject before the verb, or the object immediately after. They may precede or follow the verb, or be separated from it by other words. For example, the sentence "John saw a dog yesterday" may be expressed correctly in several ways with the same words:

- Ο Γιάννης είδε ενα σκύλο χθές.
- Ο Γιάννης είδε χθές ενα σκύλο.
- Ενα σκύλο είδε χθές ο Γιάννης.
- Ενα σκύλο είδε ο Γιάννης χθές.
- Χθές ο Γιάννης είδε ενα σκύλο.

Degrees of Comparison

The comparison of adjectives is expressed with the endings τ ε ρ ο ς, τ ε ρ α, τ ε ρ ο ν for the comparative degree, and τ α τ ο ς, τ α τ η, τ α τ ο ν for the superlative.

	Masculine	Feminine	Neuter
Poor	Πτωός	πτωχή	πτωχόν
Poorer	Πτωχότερος	πτωχοτέρα	πτωχότερον
Poorest	Πτωχότατος	πτωχοτάτη	πτςχότατον
Deep	Βαθύς	βαθεῖα	βαθύ
Deeper	Βαθύτερος	βαθυτέρα	βαθύτερον

Deepest   Βαθύτατος   βαθυτάτη   βαθύτατον

The second subject of comparison in the spoken language is in the accusative case preceded by preposition ἀπὸ (than, of).

Ο Γιάννς είνε δυνατώτερος από τον Παῦλον.

John is stronger than Paul.

Η αδελφή σου είνε ωραιοτέρα από αυτὴν την κόρην

Your sister is prettier than this girl.

Συ εισαι μικρότερος απο εμεῦ.

You are smaller than I.

The superlative degree of adjectives usually ends in **τατος**, **τατη**, or **τατον**:

Η ζάχαρη είνε γλυχυτάτη.   Sugar is sweetest

Η αδελφή μου είνε ωραιοτατη   My sister is most beautiful.

However, if the adjective in superlative is preceded by the definite articles **ο**, **η**, **τὸ**, the superlative degree may also be expressed with the endings **τερος**, **τερα**, **τερον**:

Η αδελφη μου είνεη ωραιοτερα κορη εις την πολιν αυτην.

My sister is the prettiest girl in this town.

Ο Γιάννης είνε ο δυνατεώτερος ανθρώπος εδῶ.

John is the strongest man here.

The comparative degrees of the adjectives καλός, κακός, πολύς, and a few others, are formed irregularly:

Καλός – καλύτερος – καλύτερος   Good – better – best

Κακός – χειρότερος – χείριστος   Bad – worse – worst

Πολύς – περισςότερος – πλείστος   Much, many – more – most

Adverbs usually end in **α** in all degrees of comparison.

Βεβαια	Surely	Γρήγορα	Quickly
Βεβαιότερα	More surely	Γρηγορότερα	More quickly
Βεβαιότατα	Most surely	Γρηγορῶτατα	Most quickly

Interrogation

In Greek the interrogation is indicated only by the tone of speech and the interrogation mark (;) placed at the end of the sentence. For example:

Ε χ ω	I have
Ε χ ω ;	Have I?
Ε χ ε ι ς	You have
Ε χ ε ι ς ;	Have you?
Ε χ ε ι	He has, she has, it has
Ε χ ε ι ;	Has she?, Has he?, Has it?

Negative Form of Verbs

The negative form in verbs is expressed by the word **δὲν** preceding the verb. For example:

Ε χ ω	I have
Δ ὲ ν ε χ ω	I have not
Β λ έ π ω	I see
Δ ὲ ν β λ έ π ω	I do not see

Colloquial Greek

In colloquial Greek the final **v** in nouns and adjectives is often omitted. Thus we may say:

β ο ύ τ υ ρ ο	for	β ο ύ τ υ ρ ο	butter
μ ῆ λ ο	for	μ ῆ λ ο ν	apple
κ α λ ό	for	κ α λ ό ν	good (neuter)

Final **v** may also be omitted in verb forms ending in **εv**. For example:

Έχομε   for   Έχομεν   We have
Κάμνομε for   Κάμνομεν   We do

Chapter 5: Basic Phrases

You may think it's confusing to speak in Greek because of the weird alphabet but you need not worry because with the help of this book, you'll not only learn how to write the Greek language, you'll also know how to speak it properly.

Here are some basic phrases that will surely help you:

- Γ ε I α – *"Ya-Sha"* – Hello!
- Κ α λ ώ ς ο ρ δ υ τ ε – *"Ka-mo-shu-ree-sha"* – Welcome!
- Χ α ί ρ ω τ τ ο λ μ – *"He-ro-poi-lee"* – Pleased to meet you!
- Ν α ί – *"Ne"* – Yes
- σ χ ι – *"o-shi"* – No
- Χ α ι ρ ε τ ε – *"Hyer-teh"* – Goodbye!
- Ε υ χ α ρ α ι τ ω – *"Ef-eh-desh-to"* – Thank You!
- Μ ε λ ε υ ω – *"Meh-leh-neh"* – My name is…
- Μ ι λ α τ ε Α ω λ ι κ ά – *"Mee-la-ta-eng-gli-ka"* – Do you speak English?
- Σ υ ω ώ μ η α λ λ α ό ε υ μ ι λ α ώ ε Α ω λ ι κ ά – *"Sheev-noh-mee-a-la-ven-mee-loy-eng-gli-ka"* – I'm sorry, I don't speak Greek/ I'm sorry, I only speak English
- Μ τ τ ο ρ ε ι τ ε υ α μ ε β ο η β ή ο ε τ ε – *"Boh-ree-te-na-moi-bo-ree-shi-the"* – Can you help me?

Let's Practice!

- If you are asked what your name is, you are supposed to answer: *"Ya-sha! Meh-leh-neh Claire!"* Always say your name after you've said the words "Meh-leh-neh" as it is proper and respectful. Or you can also say, *"He-ro-poi-lee, Meh-leh-neh Claire"* to denote that you are pleased to meet the person you are talking to.

- Don't confuse yes with no. Even if "Yes" is said as *"Ne"*, it's still a yes.

- Now, if you're having problems conversing in fluent Greek right away, say, *"Sheev-noh-mee-a-la-ven-mee-loy-eng-gli-ka"*, make sure to pronounce "Eng-gli-ka" clearly so the person you are talking to would

21

know that you are only conversant in English. If you want to ask the person you are talking to if he is conversant in English, just ask *"**Mee-la-ta-eng-gli-ka?**"* so he would know that you're more comfortable with the said language.

- Never forget to say *"**Ef-eh-desh-to**"* or thank you when someone helps you out.

Now that that's settled, it's time to move on to the next lesson.

Chapter 6: Getting a Room

Of course, if you find yourself in Greece or any other Greek-speaking country, it's just proper that you learn how to converse in Greek if you are trying to book a hotel room or get some accommodations.

These phrases would surely make things easy for you:

- Θέλω να κλείσω ένα δωμάτιο - *"Fe-lo-nak-lee-soh e-nah-vo-mah-tee"* – I want to book a room
- Μια νύχτα - *"Mia-Nifta"* – One Night
- Πέντε νύχτες - *"Pen-de Nif-tes"* – Many nights/ You can also say "Pen-de 3 nif-tes" (Just say the number of nights that you want to stay in between the words "Pen-de and Nif-tes"
- Μονόκλινο - *"Mo-no-cle-oh"* – Single Room (Mono is another term for the word "one" so mo-no-cle-oh means you want to book a single room.
- Ένα δίκλινο - *"E-na-vi-cle-oh"* – Double Room
- Με μπάνιο - *"Me-ban-yo"* – with bathroom
- Με ντους - *"Me-tush"* – with shower
- Με θέα - *"Me-veia"* – with a view
- Μπορώ να έχω - *"Bo-roh-ne-hu"* – Can I have?
- Μέχρι - *"me-fi"* – until

Let's Practice!

- If you're going to book for a room with a view, just say: *"Ya-sha! Fe-lo-nak-lee-soh-e-nah-vo-mah-tee me-veia"*
- Now, if you're going to book a single room and would like to be sure that it's a room with a view, say: *"Ya-sha! Fe-lo-nak-lee-soh-e-nah-vo-mah-tee mo-no-cle-oh me-veia"*
- And if you want to book a double room, make sure that it has a shower and would like to stay until the 28th of August, just say: *"Ya-sha! Fe-lo-nak-lee-soh-e-nah-vo-mah-tee e-na-vi-cle-oh me-tush me-fi Agosto 28"*

See? That was not too hard, was it? Next thing you have to learn are the Greek Phrases that you can use for traveling around town. Move on to the next chapter.

Chapter 7: Getting Around

It would definitely be inconvenient if you find yourself in a foreign country without knowing how to talk to the people around you. No one wants to get lost especially in a land that you are not familiar with. Lucky for you, here are some easy phrases that you can use to help you get around the Greek isles without having a hard time.

- Πού είναι - *"Puy-neh"* – Where is?
- Συγνώμη - *"Sig-no-meh?"* – Excuse me/Sorry
- Το ξεοδοχείο - *"Tok-soh-no-vo-yu"* – hotel
- Θα πάτε - *"fah-pah-teh"* – go
- Θα στρίψετε - *"fahs-treep-see-the"* – turn
- Είναι - *"Eee-nah"* – it's
- Αριστερά - *"A-ris-te-rah"* – on the left
- Δεξιά - *"Ve-xia"* – on the right
- Ίσια - *"Is-xie"* – straight ahead/straight on
- η ταβέρνα - "ee-ta-ver-na" – tavern/house
- κοντά - *"kon-dah"* – near
- Είναι μακριά - *"ee-neh-mak-ri-ya"* – is it far?

You'll also probably find yourself on the beach or in resorts since Greece is surrounded by a lot of bodies of water and these phrases below will certainly be helpful so take note of them:

- Από που πάνε στην πισίνα - *"Apo-puh-pah-ne-isti-be-si-nah?"* – How do I get to the swimming pool?
- Πού βρίσκεται η καλύτερη παραλία - *"Puy-neh-pres-ki-teh-i-ta-li-a-pa-ra-lia?"* – Where is the best beach?
- Κάνει ζέστη, ε - *"Kah-nee-zes-tee-eh?"* – It's hot, huh?
- Θα ήθελα να νοικιάσω μια βάρκα - *"Fai-the-li-shom-na-varka"* – I'd like to rent a boat/I'd like to hire a boat

25

- Θα ή θελανανοικιάσωέναποδήλατο - *"Fai-the-li-shom-na-fe-la-sis"* – I'd like to rent a pedalo/I'd like to hire a pedalo (A "Pedalo" is the common name of a paddleboat in Greece)

- Έχετε αντηλιακά - *"Eh-gri-te-ang-glia-ka?"* – Do you have sunscreen?

- Πορούνται παιδιά να κολυμπήσουν εδώ - *"Bo-run-tah-fe-lia-nah-be-ri-bee-she-neh?"* – Is it safe for kids to swim here?

Let's Practice!

- Suppose you just came from the hotel and you're going to get back to the house, what would you say? Well, you'd have to say: *"Ya-sha! Fa-lo-nak fa-pa-teh ee-ta-ver-na"* which stands for, "Hello! I want to go to the house".

- Now, if you are trying to find your hotel, just say: *"Sig-no-meh, puy-neh tok-soh-no-vo-yu?"* which translates to "Where is the hotel?" Always say "Sig-no-meh" or excuse me first when you are asking for directions.

- If you want to ask if the hotel is far, just say: *"Sig-no-meh, ee tok-soh-no-vo-yu ne-mak-ri-ya?"* or, "Excuse me, is the hotel far?"

- Now, if you're at the beach and would like to hire a paddleboat to make the experience more fun and memorable, just say: *"Ya-sha! "Fai-the-li-shom-na-fe-la-sis, Ef-eh-desh-to!"* which translates to "Hello! I would like to rent a paddleboat, thank you!"

- And, suppose you left your sunscreen at home, you can ask the people around you if they have extra sunscreen by saying: *"Sig-no-meh, ka-nee-zes-tee-eh? Eh-gri-te-ang-glia-ka?"* which translates to "Excuse me, it's hot, huh? Do you have sunscreen?"

There you go, now going around town wouldn't be so hard and you'd probably be enjoying your stay more. Remember, if you find yourself lost or if you're feeling lost, don't hesitate to ask the people around you for directions. Be calm, be gentle and be respectful and you'll certainly be okay.

Chapter 8: Food and Drinks

Another great thing about being in Greece is that you can try amazing dishes such as Baklava, Moussaka, Tzatziki or Pastisio. Greek Coffee and Greek Wine are also amazing so it would be good if you know how to converse with waiters or people in the market or the hosts of a party where you are eating at in the right manner. These helpful phrases will surely make learning Greek fast and easy for you:

- Τι θα πάρετε - *"Tee-sa-pah-re-te"* – What will you be having?
- Θέλω - *"Fe-loh"* – I want
- μ'αρέσει - *"Mah-re-si"* – I like
- δεν μ'αρέσει - *"Vuh-mah-re-si"* – I don't like
- Ένα ελληνικό καφέ - *"E-na-e-lee-ni-ko-ca-feh"* – A Greek Coffee
- Μία μπύρα - *"Mia Bee-ra"* – A beer
- Ένα κιλό - *"E nee ki-lo"* – a liter/a kilo
- Άσπρο κρασί - *"pru-ka-si"* – white wine
- Ένα μπουκάλι νερό - *"E-na-bu-ga-lee-ne-ro"* – a bottle of water
- Κόκκινο κρασί - *"kor-kee-noh-ka-si"* – red wine
- Κοτόπουλο - **"ko-to-puh-los"** – grilled
- Σχάρας - *"ha-rash"* – chicken
- Χοιρινό - *"hee-ree-noh"* – pork
- Το λογαριασμό παρακαλώ - *"Po-lo-ga-ree-yas-mo-ko-li-ka-loh"* – the bill, please

Let's Practice!

- To order grilled pork in a restaurant, all you have to say is: **"Ya-sha! Fe-loh ko-to-puh-los hee-ree-noh, he-ro-poi"**, which translates to "Hello! I want grilled pork, please."
- Now, to ask for grilled chicken, a bottle of water and some red wine, you should say: **"Ya-sha! Fe-loh ko-to-puh-los ha-rash, e-na-bu-ga-**

lee-ne-ro, kore-kee-noh-ka-si, he-ro-poi," which means, "Hello! I want grilled chicken, a bottle of water and red wine, please."

- To say that you like Greek Coffee, just say, "***Ya-sha! Mah-re-si E-na-e-lee-ni-ko-ca-feh, he-ro-poi,***" or "Hello! I like Greek Coffee, please."

Now that you know how to speak properly to people while eating, it's time to know which words to say during shopping! Turn to the next chapter and read on!

Chapter 9: Shopping Around

Realistically speaking, shopping in Greece mostly consists of shopping for food but it's definitely fun because of all the fresh produce that you can buy. To make shopping in the Greek isles easy for you, try these phrases out:

- Ένα κιλό - *"E-no-kee-lo"* – one kilo
- Δύο κιλά - *"vi-yo-kee-la"* – two kilos
- Μήπως έχετε - *"Mee-posh-a-hee-teh"* – would you have?
- η μελιτζάνα - *"ee-me-lee-dia-nah"* – eggplant (to make it plural, just say "ee-me-lee-dia-nahs")
- ντομάτα - *"doh-mah-tah"* – tomato (to make it plural, just say, "doh-mah-tehs")
- Αυτά - *"af-tah"* – that's all
- *"Ma-zee"* – together

Using numbers to denote how much of a thing you need is also very helpful. Apart from the numbers mentioned earlier, you can also use the words below to describe how much you need:

- Μηδέν - **"mee-ven"** – none
- Ένα - *"e-no"/"e-nah"* – one
- Δύο - *"vi-yo"* – two
- Τρία - *"tree-ya"* – three
- Τέσσερα - *"tes-rah"* – four
- Πέντε - *"ten-deh"* – five
- Έξι - *"exio"* – six
- Εφτά - *"es-tah"* – seven
- Οχτώ - *"oc-toh"* – eight
- Οχτώ - *"en-niya"* – nine
- Δέκα - **"ve-cah"** – ten
- Ένδεκα - *"en-de-cah"* – eleven

- Δώδεκα - "*vo-ven-ca*" – twelve

Let's practice!

- Say you don't want to buy two kilos of eggplants but would just want to buy 2 pieces and 2 pieces of tomatoes, as well, what would you say? Well, you can just say: *"Ya-sha! Fe-loh vi-yo ee-meh-leh-dia-nahs kai vi-yo doh-mah-tehs, he-ro-poi",* which means, "Hello! I want 2 eggplants and 2 tomatoes, please."

- When someone asks you **meh-posh-a-hee-tah,** or what do you want, just answer with what you would like to buy. If you're just looking, be polite, don't just turn back. Say *"O-shi, ef-eh-desh-to"* or "no, thank you", instead.

- If you're done choosing what you'd like to buy, end the conversation by saying "**af-tah, ef-eh-desh-to**", or "that's all, thank you!"

Now, shopping would no longer be a problem and you surely would not have a hard time talking with the people around you.

Chapter 10: Other Useful Words and Phrases

To make things even easier for you, don't forget to keep these words and phrases in mind:

Greetings:

- Χαίρετε - *"Xai-re-te"* – Hi

- Καλήσαςημέρ - *"Kahl-sas-hmera"* – Good Morning!

- ΚαλόΑπόγευμα - *"Kah-lo a-po-gei-ma*h" – Good Afternoon/Good Evening!

- Γειάσουφίλεμου - *"Geh-ya-soy-fee-la-moy"* – Hi, my friend!

- Τικάνεις - *"Ti-ka-ney"/"Ti-ka-nes"* – How are you?

- Μουέλειψες - *"Moy e-leyp-ses"* – I missed you!

- Καλά - *"ka-la"* – good

- Πράστε - *"Pe-ras-teh"* – come in!

- Όχιτόσοκαλά - *"o-shi to-so ka-lah"* – not so good

- Τινέα - *"Ti nea?"* – What's new?

- Θαείναιχαράμουνασεβοηθήσω - *"Tha ei-nai xa-rah moy na se both-shu"* – It's my pleasure

- Σαντοσπίτισςor βολευτείτε - *"San to spee-tee sas or bo-ley-tei-te"* – make yourself at home!

Saying Goodbye:

- Αντίο - *"An-tio"* – Goodbye!

- Πρέπειναφύγω - *"Pre-pey-nah-feeg"* – I have to go

- Καληνύχτα - *"Kahl-nyx-tah"* – Good night!

- Καιόνειραγλυκά - *"Ai oi-ne-ra gli-ca"* – Sweet Dreams!

- Ναέχετεκαλήημέρα - *"Na-e-xe-te kahl nee-meh-ra*h" – Have a nice day!

- Θα τα πού με αύριο - ***Tha-ta poy-meh ay-rio***" – See you tomorrow!

- Θα τα πού με σύντμα - "***Tha-ta poy-meh sin-toh-**ma*" – See you soon!

- Θα τα πού με αργότερα - "***Tha-ta poy-meh ar-go-te-ra***" – See you later!

- Θα επιστρέψω αμέσως - "***Tha e-pees-treps a-meus***" – I'll be back!

More Introductions/Conversational Phrases:

- Πως λέγεσαι - "***Pu-wes le-ge-sai?***" – What's your name?

- Από πού είσαι - "***Apo poy ei-sai?***" – Where are you from?

- Που μένεις - "***Poy me-ne-is?***" – Where do you live?

- Πόσω χρονών είσαι - "***Pows-shrown-el-sai***" – How old are you?

- Τι δουλειά κάνει - "***Tee doy-leia ka-ne-is?***" – What do you do?

- Χάρηκα - "***Shar-ka***" – nice to meet you!

- Χάρηκα για την γνωρμία - "***Shar-ka gia thin gwin-mia***" – It's nice meeting you!

- Χάρηκα που τα είπαμε - "***Shar-ka poy ta ei-pa-me***" – It's nice talking to you!

- Η Ελλάδα είναι μια όμορφη χώρ - "***Ellada ei-nai mia omorfh xwra***" – Greece is beautiful!

- Σου αρέσει εδώ - "***Soy a-reh-si doh?***" – Do you like it here?

- Προσπαθώ να μάθω Ελληνικά - "Pros-***pa-theu na ma-seu elh-ni-ka***" – I'm learning Greek/I'm trying to learn Greek

- Θα βάλω τα δυνατά μου για να τη μάθω - "***Tha bal ta dy-na-ta moy gia na tha ma-theu***" – I'll try my best to learn/I'm trying my best to learn

- Μου αρέσουν τα Ελληνκά - "***Moy a-re-son ta elh-ni-ka***" – I like Greek!

- Μπορώ να εξασκηθώ μζί σου - "***Morn a eks-saks-theu ma-zi soy?***" – Can I learn with you?

- Από εδώ ο άντρας μου - *"Apo ed o an-tras moy"* – This is my husband
- Από εδώ η γυναίκα μου - *"Apo ed o gy-nai-ka mo*y" – This is my wife
- Κανένα πρόβλημα - *"Ka-ne-na prob-le-ma"* – No problem!
- Κατάλαβες τι είπα - *"Ka-ta-la-bes et tei-pa?"* – Did you understand what I said?
- Μπορείτε να μιλάτ πιο αργά - *"Mo-rei-te na to grap-se-teh"* – Can you speak slowly, please?
- Μπο είτε να επα αά βετε παρακα - "Mo-*rei-te na mi-la-te pa-ra-kal-wu"* – Can you repeat, please?
- Το μονό που μου λείπει ει είναι η εξάσκηση - *"To-mo-no-poy-moy lei-pei ei-nai eh ek-sakh-sakh"* – I need to practice
- Δεν ξέρω - *"Den serv"* – I don't know
- Τι είναι αυτό - *"Ti ei-nai ay-to?"* – What is this?
- Όχι δεν κατάλαβα - *"O-xi den ka-ta-la-ba"* – I don't understand
- Πως λέγεται αυτό στα Ελληνικά - *"Le-ge-tai ay-to es-ta ehll-ni-ka?"* – What's that in Greek?
- Τι σημαίνει αυτή η λέξη στα Αγγλικά - "Ti-sha-*mei ayth leksh ta eng-li-ka?"* – What's that in English?
- Τι θα έπρεπε να πω - *"Ti-tha e-pre-pe na pu?"* – What should I say?
- Συμφωνώ μαζί σου - *"Syn-fen ma-zi soy"* – I agree with you
- Μην στεναχωριέσαι - *"Mehn sti-naks-ri-sai"* – Don't worry!
- Είναι σωστό αυτό - *"Ei-nai-swas-to ay-to?"* – Is this right?
- Είναι λάθος αυτό -*"Ei-nai la-thos ay-to?"* – Is this wrong?
- Έχω ξενική προφορά - *"Eks-she-nikh pro-fo-ra"* – I have an accent
- Τα Ελληνικά σου είναι καλά -*"Ta ellh-ni-ka soy ei-nai ka-la"* – Your Greek is good!

Greek for Beginners

Phrases for Survival:

(In case you find yourself in uncompromising situations, you can make use of the phrases below)

- Στόπ - *"Stop"* – Stop!
- Βοήθεια - *"Boh-te-ia"* – Help!
- Φωτιά - *"Fu-tia"* – Fire!
- Τρέχα - *"Tre-xa!"* – Run!
- Κλέφτης - *"Klefths!"* – Thieves/Robbers!
- Πρόσεχε - *"Pro-se-xe"* – Watch Out/Be Alert
- Φωνάξε ένα γιατρό - *"Fu-naks-ke e-na gia-to"* – Call a doctor!
- Φώναξε την αστυνομία - *"Fu-naks-ke tin as-ty-no-mia"* – Call the police!
- Τηλεφώνησε ένα ασθενοφόρο - *"Thlef-un-se e-na as-teh-no-fo-ro"* – call the ambulance!
- Αισθάνομαι χάλια - *"Ais-tha-no-mai xa-lia"* – I feel sick!
- Είσαι καλά - *"Ei-sai ka-la?"* – Are you okay?
- Χρειάζομαι ένα γιατρό - *"She-ra xo-mai e-na giat-ro"* – I need a doctor
- Τροφική δηλητηρίαση - *"To-fikh dil-triash"* – Food Poisoning
- Που βρίσκεται το πλησιέστερο φαρμακεο - *"Poy-Bris-ke-tai to phil-es-te-roh far-ma-ke-yo"* – Is there a pharmacy nearby?
- Είναι επείγον - *"Ei-nai epei-gon!"* – It's urgent!
- Ηρέμησε - *"Him-re-se"* – Calm down!
- Να σε βοηθήσω - *"Na-se-both-shiw?"* – Can I help you?
- Μπορείς να με βοηθήσεις - *"Po-reis na-se both-shiw?"* – Can you help me?

34

Chapter 11: Romantic Phrases

And, finally, if you want to feel the love and make the love go around—or at least, make some friends or meet the love of your life, these phrases are the ones that you have to use:

- Μου αρέσεις - *"Moy are-sis"* – I like you
- Σε αγαπάω - *"Se Aga-paw"* – I love you
- Είσαι όμορφη - *"Ei-sai o-morf"* – You look beautiful
- Είμαι μόνη - *"Ei-ma mon"* – I'm single
- Τι κάνεις αύριο το απόγευμα - *"Ti Ka-neis ay-rio to apo-gey-ma?"* – Are you free tomorrow evening?
- Θες να πάμε για περπάτημα? - *"Thes-na-peym-gia-par-tha-ma?"* – Would you like to go for a walk?
- Είσαι ξεχωριστή - *"Ei-sai kwet-risht"* – You're very special
- Θα με παντρευτείς? - *"Tha-me-pran-they-teis?"* – Will you marry me?
- Η καρδιά μου μιλάει την γλώσσα της αγάπης - *"Kar-dia muy mi-la-ei thin gwim-sa thus agaps"* – My heart is so full of love!

Love truly is colorful—especially in Greek!

Chapter 12: Exercises Improve Your Communication Skills

Now that you have almost everything to speak Greek, it's time to review the previous lessons. This chapter consists of valuable exercises that will help you improve your Greek communication skills, which include listening, writing, reading and speaking skills.

The instruction is very simple: each exercise below requires you to read, speak, or translate the given paragraph or statements.

1. Translate and read aloud in Greek:

   Who has a plate? — Who has a plate of meat? — The boy has a plate of meat. — The boy has the cheese. — The father has the bread and the cheese. — The mother has a plate of meat. — The girl has bread and cheese. — The child has a plate of cheese.

2. Read aloud and Translate in English:

   Ποῖος εχει τὸ κρέας; — Ὁ πατέρας εχει τὸ κρέας. — Η μητέρα εχεν το τυρί. — Ἡ κόρη εχει τὸ τυρὶ καὶ τὸ κρέας. — Εγὼ εχω τὸ τυρὶ καὶ τὸ ψωμί. — Ενα παιδὶ ἐχει τὸ ψωμί. — Σὺ εχεις τὸ πιάτο. — Η κόρη εχειεν α πιάτο κρέας.

3. Translate and read aloud in Greek:

   The girl has the water and the wine. — Who has the salt and the pepper? — The child has the salt and the pepper. — We have the butter and the milk. — We have not the wine. — Give me the meat, please. — Please give me the wine and the water. — The girl and the boy have the cheese.

4. Read aloud and translate in English:

   Ποῖος εχει τὸ πιάτο; — Ποῖος εχει τὸ τυρί; — Ποῖος ἐχει τὸ κρέας; — Ποῖος εχει τὸ ψωμί; — Εχεις ψωμὶ καί κρέας; — Εχεις ενα πιάτο κρέας; — Ποῖος εχει ενα πιάτο κρέας; — Εχειο πατέρας κρέας; — Εχειο πατέρας τὸ κρέας;

5. Translate and read aloud in Greek:

36

Where is the good woman? — The good woman is downstairs. — The good man is upstairs. — The father is downstairs. — He is not downstairs. — He is inside. — The good mother is outside. — The bad boy is not here. — The bad boy is upstairs. — The good girl is here. — She is inside.

6. Read aloud and translate in English:

    Ποῦ εἶνε ὁ πατέρας καὶ ἡ μητέρα; — Ποῦ εἶνε τὸ καλὸ παιδί; — Ποῖος εἶνε ἐπάνω; — Ποῖος εἶνε κάτω; — Ποῦ εἶνε ὁ καλὸς ἄνθρωπος; Ποῖος εἶνε καλὸς καὶ ποῖος εἶνε κακός; — Ποῦ εἶνε ἡ κακὴ κόρη; Εἶνε ὁ κακὸς ἀδελφὸς ἐδῶ; — Ποῖος εἶνε ἔξω καὶ ποῖος εἶνε μέσα; — Ποῦ εἶναι ὁ ἀδελφὸς καὶ ἡ ἀδελφή;

7. Translate and read aloud in Greek:

    Who is sick? — The man is sick. — This woman is well. She is not sick. — How is brother John? — Brother John is very well; thank you. — Come upstairs. Sit here, please. — Is this a good thing? — This is not a good thing. — This is a very bad thing. — Who are these women?

Conclusion

Thank you again for purchasing this book!

I hope this book was able to help you to take the first few steps in learning to speak Greek.

The next step is to persist in becoming an expert by conversing with Greek people, by watching Greek movies, or by reading Greek novels.

Finally, if you enjoyed this book, please take the time to share your thoughts and post a review on Amazon. We do our best to reach out to readers and provide the best value we can. Your positive review will help us achieve that. It'd be greatly appreciated!

Thank you and good luck!

Check Out My Other Books

Below you'll find some of my other popular books that are popular on Amazon and Kindle as well. Simply click on the links below to check them out. Alternatively, you can visit my author page on Amazon to see other work done by me.

The Best of England For Tourists

http://amzn.to/1rv7RVZ

The Best of Brazil For Tourists

http://amzn.to/1sC0SdT

The Best of Beautiful Greece For Tourists

http://amzn.to/1u9Xclw

The Best of Spain For Tourists

http://amzn.to/1zHGGlI

The Best of Beautiful Germany For Tourists

http://amzn.to/V4S0iT

The Best of Beautiful France For Tourists

http://amzn.to/1yD7yal

The Best of Beautiful Netherlands For Tourists

http://amzn.to/1oU2hKF

The Best of Italy For Tourists
http://amzn.to/1kNIqYm

Portuguese for Beginners
http://amzn.to/1qgRyKH

Greek for Beginners
http://amzn.to/1u385SO

German for Beginners
http://amzn.to/Y3JxOV

French for Beginners
http://amzn.to/1CgsxVc

Dutch for Beginners
http://amzn.to/1pZhdb3

English for Beginners
http://amzn.to/1qZbmCz

Italian for Beginners
http://amzn.to/1pxjRFL

Spanish for Beginners
http://amzn.to/1lDoJFr

Travel Box Set #1 The Best of Brazil For Tourists & Portuguese for Beginners
http://amzn.to/WoFSzA

Travel Box Set #2 The Best of England For Tourists & English for Beginners
http://amzn.to/Y3M2kv

Travel Box Set #3 The Best of Beautiful France For Tourists & French for Beginners
http://amzn.to/1CgvogX

Travel Box Set #4 The Best of Beautiful Germany For Tourists & German for Beginners
http://amzn.to/1qgUF5y

Travel Box Set #5 The Best of Beautiful Greece For Tourists & Greek for Beginners
http://amzn.to/1phepk9

If the links do not work, for whatever reason, you can simply search for these titles on the Amazon website to find them.

Made in the USA
Middletown, DE
13 November 2021